STARS IN
DIOR

STARS IN DIOR

RIZZOLI
NEW YORK

New York · Paris · London · Milan

This book provides a record of the *Stars en Dior, de l'écran
à la ville* exhibition presented at the Musée Christian Dior in
Granville (Normandy, France), May 12 to September 23, 2012.

General curator: Florence Müller
Associate curator: Barbara Jeauffroy-Mairet
Scenographer: Frédéric Beauclair
Curator: Brigitte Richart
Head of collections: Marie-Pierre Osmont
Coordinator: Ophélie Verstavel
Researcher: Laura Vallée
Cultural mediator: Chloé Kerhoas

Stars in Dior
Rizzoli International Publications, Inc.
300 Park Avenue South, New York, NY 10010
www.rizzoliusa.com

© 2012 Christian Dior

Preface: Serge Toubiana
Introduction: Florence Müller
Texts: Jérôme Hanover
Captions: Barbara Jeauffroy-Mairet
and Vincent Leret

Archive Photography: Laziz Hamani,
assisted by Antoine Lippens

Editorial Direction: Catherine Bonifassi, Anthony Petrillose
Art Direction: Daniel Baer
Production: Maria Pia Gramaglia
Text Editor: Caitlin Leffel

Editorial Coordination : CASSI EDITION
Vanessa Blondel, Nathalie Chapuis, Marylène Cudeville

ISBN : 978-0-8478-3927-8
Library of Congress Control Number: 2012936038

Contents

Marilyn Monroe in Dior,
photographed by Bert Stern during
the "Last sitting," Hotel Bel-Air,
Los Angeles, June 1962.

Dior and the Movies

Serge Toubiana

The photograph that shows Christian Dior delicately holding Ava Gardner by the shoulders, the coturier sumptuously draping the actress, enchants the cinematic imagination. Both are looking in the same direction, no doubt toward a mirror in which Gardner is assessing or anticipating the effect produced on her by the rough outlines of a dress that will be specially designed for her. We have the impression that Dior is protecting Gardner, that he will help her dash onto the set, into the spotlight; it is Christian Dior in the posture of a director.

The entire haute couture world is based on the idea of a mise-en-scène. Designers fashion beautiful dresses to be worn and to move with women's movements, but above all they design them to be *seen*. Not surprisingly, the connections between haute couture and the movies have always been mysterious, mesmerizing, based on a likeness in the gestures, on the same desire for beauty, on a somewhat similar artisanal economy.

The beautiful photos that illustrate this book reveal the ambience of the Christian Dior house of couture during different periods in its history. We find the same atmosphere, the same turmoil, the same disorder, the same ferment of activities as on a movie set. These photos allow us to discover the flip side: the preparation for an haute couture season, the fittings, the last gestures, the final alterations. Everyone is on the move, bustling about, right up to the runway show. Then, in that magical moment, the new designs are presented, as on a film set where the technical crew rushes around setting up the scene or shot, adjusting the lighting. The actors say their lines one last time before the clapboard snaps shut, and they all hold their breath at the ritual call of "Silence . . . action!"

Emotion and beauty come at that price: a great deal of energy and enormous teamwork, until the director takes charge again. Dior himself evokes that comparison between haute couture and the movies in his 1956 autobiography *Christian Dior et moi* (*Dior by Dior*): "If at present we can compare the couturier to a director, in Paquin's and Doucet's time, he was closer to a film producer. His job consisted of exploiting and making the most of other people's ideas."[1] Collaborators fuss over every detail, whereas the stage director conceptualizes the overall vision,

making sure that his creation is harmonious, consistent with his ideas and, especially, with his wishes. The same is true in the movies. Only the creator's eye counts, since it sees everything. His signature is lodged in the slightest detail.

Ava Gardner was not a fashion model but a movie star. Many a star passed through the hands of Christian Dior, then through those of the couturiers who succeeded him after his death in 1957. Yves Saint Laurent, Marc Bohan, Gianfranco Ferré, and John Galliano maintained a privileged relationship with the movies and with movie stars. From the start, that association was part of the House of Dior, created in 1946 after the war ended. It was a time when people started dreaming again, began believing again in happiness. "We came out of a time of war, of uniforms, of women soldiers built like boxers. I designed flower women, soft shoulders, busts in full flower, waists slender as lianas and skirts flared like corollas," Dior wrote. That says it all: here was the New Look and Dior's glory.

Haute couture took up the challenge of feminine elegance; the movies, that of telling stories that could make everyone the world over laugh and dream. A common, joint mission. Because he loved painting (let us not forget that for a time he was an art gallery owner, that he exhibited Picasso, Dalí, Calder, Giacometti, Miró), because he was close to poets and artists such as Max Jacob, Henri Sauguet, Christian Bérard, and Jean Cocteau, Christian Dior naturally pursued an association with theater, film, and the arts. Not surprisingly, he designed several costumes for *Les enfants terribles* (*The Terrible Children*), Jean-Pierre Melville's 1949 film based on Jean Cocteau's novel, including the famous striped dressing gown worn by Nicole Stéphane.

Marlene Dietrich was undoubtedly the most loyal star, both friend and client to Christian Dior, requiring in her film contracts that she be dressed in Dior onscreen. The dress she wears in Alfred Hitchcock's *Stage Fright* (1950), designed by Dior, plays an essential role in that black-and-white thriller. A white dress stained with blood: that detail reveals the sadistic desire of Hitchcock, master of suspense. The famous line attributed to the actress, "No Dior, no Dietrich," says a great deal about her loyalty to the Christian Dior label.

Rita Hayworth, Grace Kelly—first as an actress, then as a princess—Olivia de Havilland, Jayne Mansfield, Ingrid Bergman, Sophia Loren, Elizabeth Taylor, María Félix, Lauren Bacall, Gina Lollobrigida, Jane Russell, Brigitte Bardot, Jean Seberg, and Marilyn Monroe, to mention only a few, were all dressed in Dior. They wore his fashions around town—suits, skirt and coat ensembles, crêpe dresses, gowns and capes, negligees, furs, and especially evening gowns—for preview screenings, evening

Christian Dior and Ava Gardner during a fitting for *The Little Hut* (1957). In that Mark Robson film, all the actress's outfits were specially created or customized from the Christian Dior Haute Couture collection of Spring–Summer 1956.

galas, weddings, or other high society events. But they also wore them in films. "Miss Sophia Loren's Wardrobe specially created by CHRISTIAN DIOR," announced the credits for *Arabesque*, Stanley Donen's 1966 film. That same Sophia Loren, this time in *A Countess from Hong Kong*, Charlie Chaplin's last movie (1967), wore a skirt and jacket set with matching scarf and hat and, in the very beautiful ballroom scene where she dances in the arms of Marlon Brando, a long evening gown cut low in back and held up by a bow. Ingrid Bergman in *Indiscreet*, Stanley Donen's 1958 film, or in Anatole Litvak's *Goodbye Again* (1961); Olivia de Havilland in Norman Krasna's *Ambassador's Daughter* (1956); Ava Gardner, trying out the fabric for a dress she will wear in Mark Robson's *The Little Hut* (1957); Lauren Bacall dressed in Dior in Jean Negulesco's *How to Marry a Millionaire* (1953): the list of films where famous actresses are dressed in Dior goes on and on, continuing up to our own time.

Cinema and haute couture continue to coexist on good terms. Stars such as Isabelle Adjani, Penélope Cruz, Mélanie Laurent, Marion Cotillard, Nicole Kidman, Natalie Portman, and Charlize Theron, the current spokesmodel, have been or still are "ambassadors" for the House of Dior. They proudly promote the label on the red carpet of the Palais de Festivals at Cannes, becoming for an evening fashion-model-stars for what is now the most beautiful runway show in the world. What makes a house of couture endure over time? The talent of its designers, of course. Their signature style. But there is something more, something having to do with that mythical and legendary connection to the other arts, especially cinema, which is the art of movement and beauty. In that respect, the House of Dior was born under a lucky star.

Brigitte Bardot before a gala in
Germany, wearing a Concerto dress,
Christian Dior Haute Couture
collection, Fall–Winter 1956.

[1] Christian Dior, *Christian Dior et moi* (Paris: Librairie Amio-Dumont, 1956).

Dior, Couturier to the Stars

Florence Müller

In the history of twentieth-century fashion, the most remarkable aspect of Christian Dior's genius is his intuition of cinema's new and global "power of dreams" and to have contributed, through his own couture designs, toward idealizing its archetype: the movie star. As far back as 1947 and the New Look revolution, it was said that the Dior style, glamorous and sophisticated and absolutely feminine, would be the style of the stars. This book, in evoking the successive incarnations of the figure of the movie star (by turns Dior client, fashion model, and spokesmodel) wishes to pay tribute to the unique connection between a great couturier and the movies.

Christian Dior was born in 1905. In his youth, he developed a passion for the spectacle, preferring to spend his leisure time attending costume parties and charades, where he was the made-to-order costume designer for these entertaining games of dress-up. In the Roaring Twenties, Dior became passionate about avant-garde cinema and "German Expressionist films, with Conrad Veidt and Louise Brooks."[1] Once he had become a young art gallery owner, partner to Jacques Bonjean and later Pierre Colle, Christian Dior enjoyed the company of artists, musicians, and writers—all that Paris could offer him. The young Dior rubbed shoulders with the leading figures of experimental cinema. He became friends with Salvador Dalí, who was just then basking in the success of *Un chien andalou*, a film co-written by Luis Buñuel, and the cinematic scandal of 1928. Then, in his own Paris gallery, Christian Dior exhibited Dalí's work for the first time, beginning in 1931. Subsequently, he placed his talents as a designer in the service of the movies. Under the Nazi occupation, participating actively in a cinema of artistic "resistance," he excelled in the genre of costume dramas. In 1942, his name appeared in the credits for Roland Tual's *Le lit à colonnes* (*The Four-Poster*). He embarked on the career of costume design with boundless enthusiasm and astonished the film people with the creativity of his clothes. One can imagine the young Dior absorbed in history books, feasting on fashion prints and great paintings, brilliantly playing over the entire gamut of time. Without being aware of it, he was trying out the retro-style mix-and-match fashions that would make for the singularity of his famous New Look a few years later. He designed the clothes for no fewer than eight films before Dior the costume designer made way in 1947 for Dior the couturier.

His experience as a costume designer, combined with those as a fashion designer with the couturiers Robert Piguet and Lucien Lelong, prepared him for the heavy creative responsibilities at a couture house. That new, very time-consuming venture did not impel him to give up his first love, the spectacle of cinema. In Dior's mind, film and fashion may have been intimately linked, since the haute couture collections naturally possess all the glamour required for stars of the silver screen, who in turn inspired him. Some of the haute couture designs were modified a bit, but many were simply made to the actresses' measurements. Production departments and actresses were delighted. Within a few years, the avenue Montaigne label became the one that actresses and women the world over dreamed of wearing. Dior clothes showed off an ideal body conceived on the principle of a textile architecture, with its carefully calculated cut, or "line." That is exactly what was needed to showcase the stars' figures. Dior allowed them to be in sync with the dominant postwar aesthetic, that of the ultrafeminine woman, soon to be personified by Marilyn Monroe.

Dior's film wardrobe created a woman designed as a larger-than-life character. The outfits worn by Ingrid Bergman, Ava Gardner, Sophia Loren, Lauren Bacall, and Monica Bellucci placed the emphasis on their strength or impetuousness. The emblematic suit of the House of Dior, with its narrow waist, prominent bustline, and hip-hugging skirt, established the archetype for the sophisticated woman. That image of the lady of Paris lent itself to the measurements of Marlene Dietrich, Ava Gardner, Nicole Stéphane, and even Jennifer Jones. Dior lipstick took on expressionist overtones when it complemented scenes of psychological drama in Jean-Jacques Beineix's *La lune dans le caniveau* (*Moon in the Gutter*; 1983), Benoît Jacquot's *Corps et biens* (*With All Hands*; 1986), or Pedro Almodóvar's *Los abrazos rotos* (*Broken Embraces*; 2009). The sheer dresses worn by Sophia Loren in *Arabesque* (1966) and by Leslie Caron in *L'homme qui aimait les femmes* (*The Man Who Loved Women*; 1977) heralded seduction scenes. The extremely low-cut sheath evening gowns of Sophia Loren or Brigitte Bardot undressed the stars. The gray, black, beige, or white palette typical of Dior day dresses stripped away the allure of Sydne Rome, Catherine Deneuve, Mireille Darc, Stéphane Audran, and Fanny Ardant. For the roles of young girls, a very "Miss Dior" style captured the characters played by Mylène Demongeot.

In the nineteenth century, stage actresses imposed their couturiers on their directors. The audience went to the theater as if to a fashion runway show. The movies capitalized on that principle, dictating a model of elegance to millions of women.

Hollywood producers—often former fashion professionals themselves—promoted the new fashions, hairstyles, and makeup. Copies of stars' dresses were distributed through a large sales network relayed by specialized magazines. Marlene Dietrich, coming out of the years when the art of the pose counted more than that of the performance, erected no barriers between her screen image and her image around town. She started out as a client seeking to modernize her image, ultimately becoming Dior's intimate friend, part of the circle of weekend guests at Milly-la-Forêt, where Christian Dior owned a country house. She imposed Dior on Alfred Hitchcock for the costumes of *Stage Fright* (1950). The Deutsche Kinemathek in Berlin houses precious examples of Dietrich's designer wardrobe: Dior fashions worn in films, others worn in private life, many accessories, perfumes, and makeup. The *Stars in Dior* exhibition (at the Christian Dior Museum in Granville, May 12 to September 23, 2012) displays a large selection, thanks to the loan from the Kinemathek and its director, Werner Sudendorf.

The quiet surroundings and the decoration of the building at 30, avenue Montaigne, also figures in several films. Christian Dior's consent brought a film additional prestige, "what the Americans call 'production value.'"[2] The world of Dior is de rigueur whenever there is a need to evoke Paris, City of Light. Along with the Eiffel Tower, the house is one of the universal symbols of Paris. Its evocation onscreen unlocks the door to the universe of the art of living and of luxury. The House of Dior, symbol of luxury and elegance, is exploited in dialogue from Jean-Luc Godard's *À bout de souffle* (*Breathless*; 1960) and in many scenes shot at the Dior boutique (Étienne Chatiliez's *La confiance règne* [*Confidence Reigns*; 2003], Gad Elmaleh's *Coco* [2009], and Jérôme Savary's *Mistinguett, la dernière revue* [2001]). Marc Bohan plays himself in a scene from Jules Dassin's *Phaedra* (1961), as does John Galliano in Claude Lelouch's *Les Parisiens* (*The Parisians*). In *L'ours et la poupée* (*The Bear and the Doll*; 1970), Michel Deville contrasts the sophistication of Brigitte Bardot leaving the Dior boutique to the country ways of Jean-Pierre Cassel living off by himself in the sticks.

Dior costumes contribute as much to the development and expression of a character as the performance of the actress playing her. In *Tout feu, tout flamme* (*All Fired Up*; 1981), Isabelle Adjani's staid dresses and suits express the cold temperament of a young Polytech student dealing with a capricious father, played by Yves Montand. In Claude Lelouch's *Les Parisiens*, the fashion photo session, the runway show, and the dress fittings at the Dior boutique symbolize the meteoric rise of Maïwenn, a singing star. Nicole Stéphane's dressing gown in *Les enfants terribles* (*The Terrible Children*; 1950) carries all the negative charge of being housebound. Through its expression of a rejection of the outside world and confinement within the world of childhood, that article of clothing fleshes out the neurotic character of Elisabeth. That legendary costume, displayed in the *Stars in Dior* exhibition, is part of a large selection of costumes, posters, drawings, and photos lent by the Cinémathèque Française, with the enthusiastic cooporation of its director, Serge Toubiana, who kindly agreed to write the introduction to this book.

The actress client knows how to play the perfect fashion model. That cross-marketing of cinema and fashion works to the benefit of magazines, studios, and the couturier. In 1954, United Artists held a photo session depicting Christian Dior in the company of Jane Russell, who was wearing the Mazette suit. The image was publicity for the film *Gentlemen Marry Brunettes* (1955), while at the same time the House of Dior was defending itself against criticism directed at the collection of the moment, the famous H line, nicknamed the Haricot (string bean) line. The press release notes that Jane Russell ought to persuade "Hollywood stars" that "the H line does not flatten out the bust but rather supports it."[3] A series of images immortalizing the legendary beauty of Marilyn Monroe, idealized through the refinement of a very low-cut black dress, survives from the last photo session she granted to Bert Stern.

The star's influence in the media landscape is now amplified, as a result of her appearance in commercials and on the red carpet. Sharon Stone, Charlize Theron, Natalie Portman, Marion Cotillard, and Mélanie Laurent surpass runway models in their power of seduction. The directors Ridley Scott, David Lynch, Wong Kar-wai, Sofia Coppola, and Jean-Jacques Annaud cast their unique creative gaze on the universe of the House of Dior. "Cinema is the art of making pretty women do pretty things," said François Truffaut. With Dior, that promise has been fulfilled for several decades. From one film to another, from the front row of the runway show to the red carpet, movie wardrobes celebrate the star in Dior.

[1] Christian Dior, *Christian Dior et moi* (Paris: Librairie Amio-Dumont, 1956), p. 208
[2] Denise Tual, *Au coeur de temps* (Paris: Édition Carrère, 1987), p. 352.
[3] Press release from M. de Maussabré, October 14, 1954.

STARS ON THE TOWN

In February 1947, Christian Dior's first haute couture runway show introduced the New Look. In an instant, the way women had been dressing seemed out of fashion. Dior defined a new silhouette in which postwar restrictions vanished under imposing lengths of fabric, and restored peace and happiness exalted an utterly shapely femininity, the En 8 line. Actresses were among Dior's first clients. Dressed, perfumed, and made up in Christian Dior, they demanded a new glamour.

Dior in Glamorama

The scene: Dallas, 1947. Christian Dior receives the highest honor in American fashion, the Neiman Marcus Award, called the "Oscar of fashion." This illustrates the close connections between fashion and cinema west of the Atlantic. When he undertakes that journey—crossing the ocean on the *Queen Elizabeth*, traveling across the United States from New York to Hollywood, passing through Texas—he humorously compares himself to the dramatist Eugène Labiche's character Monsieur Perrichon, a respectable French bourgeois drawn into a series of unlikely predicaments during a family trip to the Alps.[1] This was not false humility: in 1947, the number of collections that Christian Dior had presented amounted to—one. Nine years later, he would write: "I smile today at the thought that those who spoke about the House of Christian Dior as a sanctified Paris attraction, equal to the Eiffel Tower and the French can-can, forgot that, at the time, it had been in existence for six months!"[2] But his sole haute couture collection, presented in Paris at the start of the year, had gone off like a bomb. "It's such a new look," exclaimed Carmel Snow, editor in chief of *Harper's Bazaar*, using an expression that would go down in history. In fact, the New Look, more than a new fashion, was a new vision of the female body, a redefinition of glamour. It celebrated a femininity taken to the extreme, a silhouette that was all bust and hips, a sexual couture. Colette summed it up: "With a thrust of the pelvis, the 'nioulouk' reconquered America."[3]

Let us return to Dallas in September 1947: "In the late afternoon, during a fitting, I had gotten tangled up in the fasteners and folds of the fabric and had exhausted myself persuading my interlocutors that the ample cleavage of the evening gowns constituted their principal attraction and novelty. Marilyn Monroe's career had not yet taken off, and everyone was looking at me in terror."[4] Let us recall the context. After World War II, Hollywood glamour consisted of a cold, ambiguous beauty. The *femme* was *fatale*, of course, but at a distance. It was a beauty in black and white, Greta Garbo or Marlene Dietrich, whereas that "ample cleavage" described by Christian Dior defined the shape of a seduction that was wholly of the flesh. A more physical, unrestrained glamour, that of Sophia Loren or Marilyn Monroe. In 1947, however, though the couturier was already a superstar, neither of these actresses was as yet famous. And there really was something terrifying about that ultrasexual glamour, as Christian Dior said at the time, for the stars who belonged to a different time and who still could not make out what was revolutionary about it. It is as if the New Look, preceding the arrival of Sophia Loren and Marilyn Monroe on the big screen, had in some sense anticipated it, called it forth, and legitimated it a priori.

What is glamour? In the collective unconscious, it is intimately linked to the movies, to actresses on the red carpet. If we trace back the word's etymology, we find it is closely related to "grammar." Both stem from the Greek *grammatikē*: culture, erudition. Glamour is above all a corporeal syntax, the totality of elements constitutive of femininity. Its definition has evolved with the era, the fashion, the star, though in the end it is not possible to say which influenced which. Just eighteen years had elapsed between Joseph von Sternberg's *Shanghai Express* (1932) and Alfred Hitchcock's *Stage Fright* (1950). Christian Dior had opened his house of haute couture, and Marlene Dietrich had become a client and a close friend: they spent their weekends together on the couturier's property in Milly-la-Forêt. Marlene Dietrich's glamour in the 1930s was not altogether the same as her glamour in the 1950s. In her attitude—especially as it is displayed in the photos of the time—there may have been a bit more mischief in the 1930s, a bit more lasciviousness in the 1950s. A certain sexual maturity. Then came Marilyn Monroe, Sophia Loren, Gina Lollobrigida, Elizabeth Taylor, Jane Russell, Brigitte Bardot, Ursula Andress, Claudia Cardinale, and all the glamour of the 1950s and 1960s.

That aesthetics of femininity, moreover, is intimately linked to fashion, because it is in magazines that the fashions are depicted. Marilyn Monroe, who began her career as a model in the 1940s, posed for the last time in 1962, six weeks before she died, for photographs taken by Bert Stern for American *Vogue*. That series, published posthumously as a tribute to the star, had in fact been conceived as a fashion shoot, and, as Stern has said, the emphasis was placed on the fashions of the couturiers of the time, for example, the two "signature Dior" black dresses. Lauren Bacall was also a fashion model before becoming an actress. And Monica Bellucci, before making her first films,

OPPOSITE
Marlene Dietrich poses for Horst P. Horst (American *Vogue*, December 1, 1947). The actress liked to refashion her outfits by switching off tops and bottoms, as, for example, with the Chandernagor ensemble, Christian Dior Haute Couture collection, Fall–Winter 1947. Originally, it had a black wool top with pale rubies embroidered by Hurel, but on that day she preferred to wear a top of her choice.

FOLLOWING SPREAD
Marilyn Monroe plays fashion model for photographer Bert Stern at the Hotel Bel-Air in Los Angeles, 1962. The series of photos will appear posthumously in American *Vogue* in September 1962

posed for the Dior makeup advertising campaign in 1990. But the proximity between magazines and actresses goes even further. Audrey Hepburn, though never a fashion model, found it amusing to play one in a series of photos for *Harper's Bazaar* in 1959. Reprising her role from two years earlier in Stanley Donen's *Funny Face* (1957), where she had played a fashion model being photographed in Paris by Fred Astaire, she posed for Richard Avedon alongside other stars of the time: Annette Stroyberg, Mel Ferrer, Buster Keaton, Zsa Zsa Gabor. In two of these shots, Audrey Hepburn is wearing fashion designs by Yves Saint Laurent, successor to Christian Dior as head of the house following Dior's death.

The interest is threefold: the actresses want to present themselves as style icons and thus legitimate their glamour, constructing a Hollywood myth; the houses of couture want to connect a public image to their brand; and the magazines want to bring a certain aura to their fashion vision. In fact, except in the 1980s, when supermodels replaced stars on magazine covers and in photo shoots, actresses have always been the best fashion vehicles. Today, their names are Mila Kunis, Natalie Portman, Marion Cotillard, Charlize Theron. They are defining a new, more natural glamour. More active as well: the female object has been replaced by the female subject.

[1] Eugène Labiche, *Le voyage de Monsieur Perrichon* (Paris: Gallimard, 2002).
[2] Christian Dior, *Christian Dior et moi* (Paris: Librairie Amio-Dumont, 1956).
[3] Colette, *Colette et la mode*, èditions Plume, 1991, p185.
[4] Christian Dior, *Christian Dior et moi*, op. cit.

PREVIOUS SPREAD
Elizabeth Taylor in a Soirée à Rio gown receiving the Oscar for Best Actress for her role in *Butterfield 8*, 1961.

ABOVE AND OPPOSITE
Elizabeth Taylor in a Diorissimo dress, Christian Dior Haute Couture collection by Marc Bohan, Spring–Summer 1961, at the premiere of a show featuring her husband, the singer Eddie Fisher, in Las Vegas, May 1961.

Humphrey Bogart and Lauren Bacall
at the Oscars in 1952. She is wearing
the Pantomime gown, Christian Dior
Haute Couture collection,
Spring–Summer 1951.

Sharon Stone, photographed
by Emanuele Scorceletti, at a photo
shoot with Jean-Baptiste Mondino
for Dior, 2006.

ABOVE AND OPPOSITE
Monica Bellucci shooting the
Rouge Dior commercial directed
by Rob Marshall, 2006.

Charlize Theron, photographed
by Alexi Lubomirski, wearing a dress
inspired by a design from the Christian
Dior Prêt-à-porter collection by
John Galliano, Fall-Winter 2008.

FOLLOWING SPREAD
Carey Mulligan, photographed by
Peter Lindbergh, in an organza and
hand-painted tulle dress from the
Christian Dior Haute Couture collection
by John Galliano, Fall–Winter 2010
(American *Vogue*, October 2010).

OPPOSITE
Marion Cotillard, photographed by
Jan Welters, wearing a black wool
jacket, Christian Dior Haute Couture
collection by John Galliano,
Fall–Winter 2010 (French *Elle*,
October 2010).

Anne Hathaway, photographed by Mario Sorrenti, wearing an embroidered ecru horsehair and silk dress, Christian Dior Haute Couture collection by John Galliano, Fall–Winter 2008 (*W*, October 2010).

Natalie Portman, photographed
by Frederic Auerbach, 2012.

Natalie Portman, photographed by Alexi Lubomirski, wearing an embroidered silk dress, Christian Dior Prêt-à-porter collection, Fall–Winter 2009.

Jennifer Garner, photographed by
Craig McDean, wearing an embroidered
orange tulle dress over trompe l'oeil flesh-
colored slip, Christian Dior Prêt-à-porter
collection by John Galliano, Spring–
Summer 2010 (*W*, January 2010).

Taking Stock

Christian Dior was still almost an unknown, his name barely whispered in Paris, though the fashion world did remember the drawings he had submitted to *Le Figaro* before the war, and some haute couture clients also recalled that he was Lucien Lelong's assistant. And yet, at his first runway show of February 1947, Marlene Dietrich was in attendance. She came as a neighbor: she lived on avenue Montaigne, next to the Bar des Théâtres. But she came as a friend, she and Dior being two of Jean Cocteau's intimates. She would choose the Chandernagor design, a dress from the Corolle line with a wide re-embroidered neckline; then Saphir, with its slit skirt; Précieuse, with double-breasted Bar jacket cinched at the waist; and Cygne Noir, for which she would have a second bodice made, slightly different from the runway design. A great deal of haute couture, of course, but also pajamas, caps, dressing gowns. And stockings: in 1954, Dietrich would become the spokesmodel for that line of lingerie. For her lips, two Dior lipsticks, numbers 28 and 5, which she would have delivered regularly to her home. Although she probably wore Miss Dior for a time—it was likely offered to her during the first runway show—she would later choose Diorama, launched in 1949, perhaps in part for the connection that the fragrance's name established with the world of the "seventh art." Louis Daguerre's diorama, a precursor to cinema, had created the illusion of a moving image.

In 1955, Olivia de Havilland, whose fragrance of choice was Eau Fraîche—and later Diorissimo—married Pierre Galante, head of the magazine *Paris Match*, in an afternoon gown and long paletot, the ligne A. Soirée de Réveillon and Soirée de Londres, the dresses she wore in *The Ambassador's Daughter* (1956), came from the same collection. She would remain a client of the house after Christian Dior's death. De Havilland wore a day suit around town and Marc Bohan evening gowns for the big movie events: a taffeta-print Nuit de Grenade for the Academy Awards ceremony in 1960, a Soirée à Rio for the *Gone with the Wind* Civil War centennial in Atlanta in 1961, a Priscilla at the San Francisco International Film Festival in 1965, and a Framboisine for the London premiere of Walter Grauman's *Lady in a Cage* (1964).

For the announcement of her engagement to Prince Rainier of Monaco, Grace Kelly wore a special creation from Christian Dior New York. In her life as a princess, with the social obligations it entailed, she would wear a white guipure dress at the Bal des Petits Lits Blancs (1966), another in multicolored *bayadère* silk chiffon at the Red Cross ball (1968), and one in coral jersey with a gold bezel for the Les Coiffes dinner (1969). She would wear more than twenty haute couture designs at the different charity events of the principality. Her connections with the house were so close that she sponsored the launch of the Baby Dior line in 1967: Caroline was ten years old at the time, Albert, nine, and Stéphanie, two.

For Stanley Donen's *Arabesque* (1966), Charlie Chaplin's *A Countess from Hong Kong* (1967), and Andrè Cayatte *Verdict* (1974), Sophia Loren insisted on being dressed in Dior. Marc Bohan was the couturier of the house at the time and a close friend of the actress. He often designed special creations for her to wear around town and onscreen. Her perfume: Miss Dior. Her makeup obsession: the marron glacé eyebrow pencil. In *Prêt-à-porter*, Robert Altman's 1994 farce about the fashion world, she played the widow of a fictional president of the Paris haute couture trade association. She attended the Dior runway show dressed in Dior, and throughout the film showcased her official wardrobe: Bar jacket with large bow tie, silk crêpe dress with polka-dot collar, strapless organza gown with draping in front.

The list goes on and on: Elizabeth Taylor and her eighteen fashion designs specially created for the film *Secret Ceremony* (1968); Marilyn Monroe and her twenty-five pairs of shoes, all picked out the same day; María Félix, Isabelle Adjani . . . to name just a few.

Grace Kelly in a Christian Dior New York gown, flanked by Alfred Hitchcock and James Stewart, at the premiere of *Rear Window* in 1954.

54

Grace Kelly in a white satin dress,
photographed by Elliott Erwitt at
the ball celebrating her engagement
at the Waldorf Astoria, New York,
January 6, 1956.

Princess Grace of Monaco,
photographed by Howell Conant,
on her tenth wedding anniversary in
1966. She is wearing a Christian Dior
special creation by Marc Bohan,
in ivory silk with stylized veined-
leaf motifs in gold lamé.

Princess Grace of Monaco during
the shooting of the documentary *A Look
at Monaco*, in silk chiffon dress with
multicolor *bayadère* motif, Christian Dior
Haute Couture collection by Marc Bohan,
Spring–Summer 1967.

ABOVE
Grace Kelly, photographed by Yousuf
Karsh, in a Colinette dress, Christian
Dior Haute Couture collection,
Fall–Winter 1956.

OPPOSITE
Princess Grace of Monaco and Marc
Bohan at the opening of the Baby Dior
boutique in 1967. She is wearing the
San Francisco suit, Christian Dior Haute
Couture collection by Marc Bohan,
Fall–Winter 1965.

ABOVE
Pregnant with her daughter Caroline,
Princess Grace of Monaco wears
a Colinette dress under a short
version of the Bal de Printemps coat,
in straw-yellow silk embroidered
with multicolor flowers by Rébé,
Christian Dior Haute Couture
collection, Spring–Summer 1956.

OPPOSITE
Bal de Printemps ensemble in straw-
yellow silk, Christian Dior Haute
Couture collection, Fall–Winter 1956.

PREVIOUS PAGE, LEFT
Eighteenth-century Chinese box given
to Her Serene Highness Princess
Grace of Monaco in 1961 by Christian
Dior Parfums during the Red Cross
gala. This box contained a Grand Luxe
edition of Diorissimo, a set of bath oils,
and an assortment of fourteen lipsticks.

PREVIOUS PAGE, RIGHT
Diorissimo bottle, Grand Luxe
edition designed by Christian Dior,
made of Baccarat crystal, flower
stopper gilded in fine gold, 1956.

OPPOSITE AND ABOVE
Ingrid Bergman during a fitting for
Indiscreet (1958). In this Stanley Donen
film, the actress wears a Tuileries
dress, Christian Dior Haute Couture
collection, Fall–Winter 1957.

ABOVE
Olivia de Havilland, a major client
of the House of Dior, tries on the
Bruxelles evening gown at the atelier,
photographed by Willy Maywald, 1954.

OPPOSITE
Bruxelles evening gown in white
guipure, Christian Dior Haute Couture
collection, Spring–Summer 1954.

Jane Russell next to Christian Dior, during a shoot organized by the House of Dior and United Artists to promote the film *Gentlemen Marry Brunettes* (1955). She will prove that the H line does not flatten figures. She is wearing the Mazette ensemble in black wool trimmed with farmed mink fur, Christian Dior Haute Couture collection, Fall–Winter 1954.

OPPOSITE
Mazette ensemble in black wool trimmed with farmed mink fur, Christian Dior Haute couture collection, Fall–Winter 1954.

ABOVE
Rita Hayworth, photographed by
Willy Rizzo in the salons of the House
of Dior, about 1950. From the first
Christian Dior collection in February
1947, the actress ordered a dozen styles,
including Maxim's, Femina, Amour,
1947, Gag, and Pompon. During the
gala for the 1946 film *Gilda*, she dazzled
Hollywood in a customized Soirée
evening gown in beige organza with
white polka dots.

OPPOSITE
Pompon suit in black wool composed
of a jacket embroidered with a fringe
of small pompons and passementerie,
and a straight skirt with the same
fringe along the hemline, Christian Dior
Haute Couture collection, Spring–
Summer 1947.

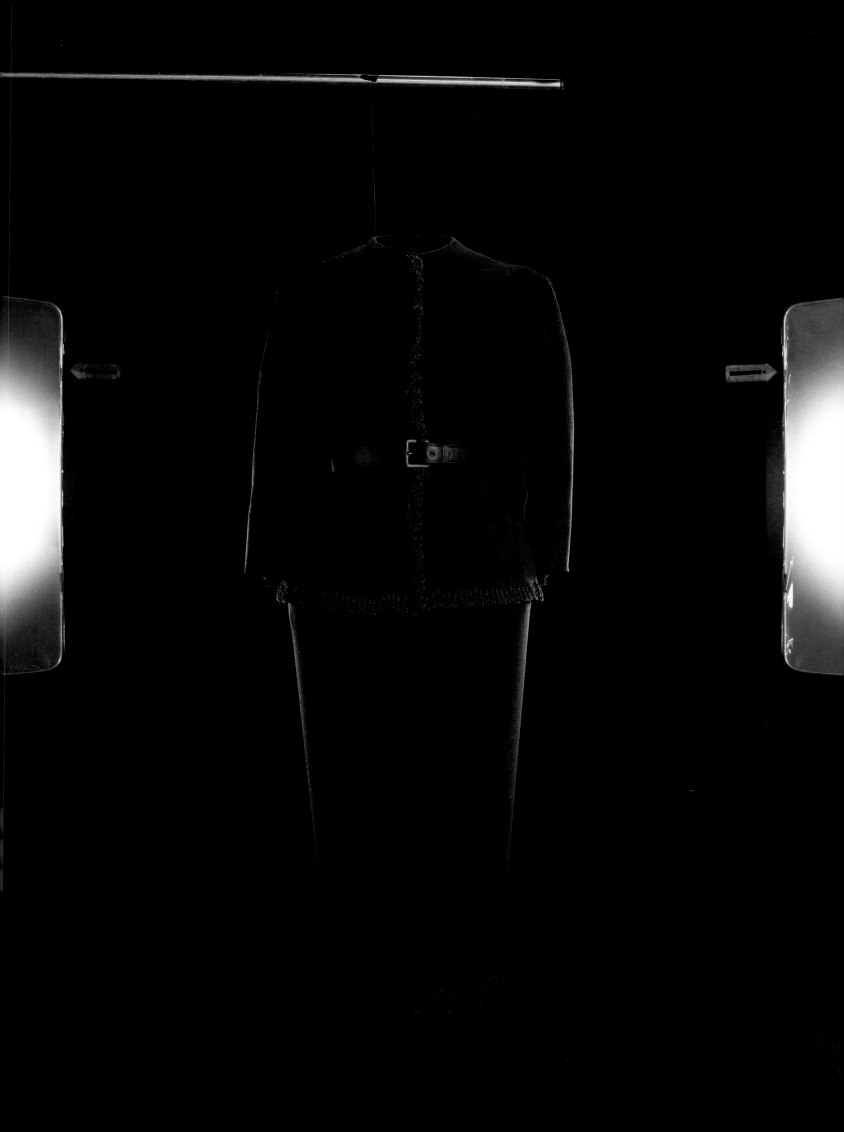

OPPOSITE
Marlene Dietrich, photographed
by Willy Rizzo in Cannes, 1955.

ABOVE
Marlene Dietrich and Willy Rizzo
in Cannes, 1955.

Miss Dior box, frosted glass
bottle decorated with houndstooth
motif in bas relief, 1950.

ABOVE
Gina Lollobrigida in the Christian Dior
London boutique, September 3, 1963,
trying on the Nuit Boréale dress created
for the Basil Dearden film *Woman of
Straw* (1964).

OPPOSITE
Nuit Boréale dress in silk faille,
Christian Dior London collection,
Spring–Summer 1963.

OPPOSITE
Eau Fraîche, clear glass bottle
adorned with a black bow around
the stopper, 1955.

ABOVE
On a stopover in Paris, Kim Novak
discovers the latest fragrances created
by the House of Dior at the boutique
on 30, avenue Montaigne, around 1960.

PREVIOUS SPREAD
Sophia Loren and her husband, the
producer Carlo Ponti, during fittings
in the salons of the House of Dior,
around 1960.

ABOVE
Sophia Loren in the boutique on avenue
Montaigne, where she has just received
a limited edition of Miss Dior in clear
Baccarat crystal bottle, around 1961.

OPPOSITE
Amphora-shaped bottle for the
Miss Dior fragrance, replicating
the lines of the first New Look
designs, of 1947.

Black gabardine suit with
turned-up sleeves, large bow around
the neck, and detachable cuffs in black
organza with white polka dots, created
specially by Gianfranco Ferré for
Sophia Loren, for the Robert Altman
film *Prêt-à-porter* (1994).

Sophia Loren with Marc Bohan
during a fitting at the Dior boutique,
February 12, 1963.

Sophia Loren and Marc Bohan with the
Dior models after the Haute Couture
runway show, Spring–Summer 1963.

ABOVE
In Jean-Luc Godard's *À bout de souffle*
(*Breathless*, 1960), the Christian Dior
boutique serves as a setting. There
Jean Seberg will find a strapless cocktail
dress, in which she will later be
photographed outside the boutique.

OPPOSITE
Floral-print strapless cocktail
dress, Christian Dior boutique,
about 1960.

PREVIOUS SPREAD
Brigitte Bardot at 30, avenue
Montaigne, receiving the Grand Luxe
edition of the Diorissimo perfume
in clear Baccarat crystal, 1959.

OPPOSITE
Brigitte Bardot in the salons of the
House of Dior, wearing a design from
the Christian Dior Haute Couture
collection by Yves Saint Laurent, 1960.

Brigitte Bardot poses in the Nuit aux Antilles ensemble, Christian Dior Haute Couture collection by Yves Saint Laurent, Spring–Summer 1960.

Jayne Mansfield in the salons of the House of Dior, wearing a Calypso dress, Christian Dior Haute Couture collection, Fall–Winter 1957.

STARS & RED CARPET

Premieres or preview screenings, charity galas or launch parties, award ceremonies, international festivals, and other society occasions: the events connected to the world of film are inescapable fashion opportunities. They are a chance for the stars to show they have style, to show they have taste, and sometimes to also show they have a special relationship with a house of couture, such as Dior. They thereby construct an image and play their role as "Star," always themselves but already performing.

Charlize Theron, photographed
by Patrick Demarchelier in her gown
specially designed for the 2012 Golden
Globe Awards, Christian Dior
Haute Couture special creation.

Nicole Kidman wears the Absinthe gown to the 1997 Academy Awards, Christian Dior Haute Couture collection by John Galliano, Spring–Summer 1997.

Tilda Swinton at the 2008 Orange British Academy Film Awards, wearing a design from the Christian Dior Haute Couture collection by John Galliano, Spring–Summer 2008.

Black tulle and blue embroidery
dress, Christian Dior Haute Couture
collection by John Galliano,
Fall–Winter 2008.

Monica Bellucci at the 2009 Cannes
Film Festival, wearing a Christian Dior
Haute Couture special creation.

Natalie Portman at the 2012 Academy
Awards, wearing a Nuit de Feu evening
gown, Christian Dior Haute Couture
collection, Spring–Summer 1954.

Penélope Cruz at the 2003 Cannes
Film Festival, wearing a special
creation adapted from a design from
the Christian Dior Haute Couture
collection by John Galliano,
Spring–Summer 2002.

Mélanie Laurent, mistress of ceremony for
the 2011 Cannes Film Festival, wears
a special creation inspired by the Diorama
design, Christian Dior Haute Couture
collection, Spring–Summer 1951.

Special creation inspired
by the Diorama evening gown,
in black silk embroidered with black
horsehair on pink background,
Christian Dior Haute Couture
collection, Spring–Summer 1951.

Nicole Kidman at the 2011 Oscars,
wearing a design from the Christian
Dior Haute Couture collection by
John Galliano, Spring–Summer 2009.

Reese Witherspoon at the 2006
Oscars, wearing a Fête à Trianon
gown, Christian Dior Haute Couture
collection, Spring–Summer 1955.

Gold lamé strapless gown,
Christian Dior Prêt-à-porter
collection by John Galliano,
Spring–Summer 2003.

rew Barrymore at the 2007 Golden
obes, wearing a special creation
spired by a design from the Christian
or Haute Couture collection by
hn Galliano, Fall–Winter 2006.

Charlize Theron at the 2012 Golden
Globes, wearing a Christian Dior
Haute Couture special creation.

Strapless evening gown in ivory
tulle and silk satin, Christian Dior
Prêt-à-porter collection by
John Galliano, Fall–Winter 2004.

STARS & THE STAGE

Dior had many actresses as clients, and it was natural for these stars to ask their directors for —even demand—Christian Dior creations for their appearances onscreen: Marlene Dietrich from Alfred Hitchcock, Sophia Loren from Stanley Donen, Ava Gardner from Mark Robson, and so on. Beyond his role as couturier-costumier, which film credits often prominently display, Dior is also a symbol; and, because of what it represents about Paris, fashion, and luxury in the American collective imagination, the name "Dior" itself serves as a setting, even a plot device in the scripts of Hollywood movies.

The Confusion of Genres

"It was A.D. 1947. . . . The new postwar years began with balls. Christian Bérard organized the *bal du Panache*, where all things bird of paradise, ostrich, and egret were gathered together on the prettiest heads in the world. Then came the *bal des Oiseaux* (Bird Ball), with feather masks lending an added mystery to the women's faces. . . . Caught up in a frenzy, everyone wanted to give a ball for a charity or for friends, in Paris, out in the country, on the Eiffel Tower, on a *bateau-mouche* in the Seine, wherever it was unusual to be dancing. Paris had once again become cosmopolitan." So we read in Christian Dior's autobiography, *Christian Dior et moi.* For these balls, the couturier was a costumier—a costume designer. The women he dressed for their goings around town came to him for these lavish high society parties. In fact, the Dior silhouette, with its highly defined waist and oversized skirt and bustline, naturally called for stage costumes: an aesthetic of excess, pushed to the extreme.

These balls were theater, and the guests were its stars. Daisy Fellowes, for example, played a fictional queen supposedly symbolizing America at the party Charles de Beistegui threw at the Palazzo Labia in Venice: "Watteau's *fêtes galantes*, Marivaux's harlequins, beautiful masks from the commedia dell'arte, Francesco Guardi's tricorn and bauta hats, cliché Chinamen . . . powdered wigs, and baskets with silks covered in gold chevrons."[1] That *bal du siècle* (ball of the century), though it was in town, would not have been upstaged by the costumes for the biggest Hollywood productions. Paradoxically, Christian Dior designed relatively few actual movie costumes, with the exception of those in period films (Roland Tual's *Le lit à colonnes* [*The Four Poster*] in 1942; Marcel Achard's *La valse de Paris* [*Paris Waltz*] in 1950). For the most part, the clothes found onscreen were selected directly from his collections. But that approach was probably not dictated by the couturier's personal taste, since, before the House of Dior was founded in 1946, he had been a costume designer for many films, dressing, notably, Odette Joyeux in Claude Autant-Lara's *Sylvie et le Fantôme* (*Sylvie and the Phantom*; 1946) and Renée Saint-Cyr in Pierre de Hèrain's *Paméla ou l'Enigme du temple* (*Pamela, or The Riddle of the Temple*, 1944). The reason was more likely a lack of time: nothing is more time-consuming than haute couture! Then, too, there was the idea Dior had of his work as a whole: "It would have been impossible for me to do an entirely new dress outside of a collection, since a design must be part of a totality,"[2] he explained. The preference of the actresses might also be mentioned, since they could thereby more easily keep their costumes and continue to dress in Dior when they were offscreen.

Indeed, all the stars were clamoring for Dior! For *Stage Fright* (1950), Marlene Dietrich, a close friend of the couturier, forced the designer on Alfred Hitchcock. "No Dior, no Dietrich," she told the production department, sure of herself, before patiently choosing her outfits from the Christian Dior Haute Couture Collection Spring–Summer 1949. That led the director to say, after shooting the film: "Miss Dietrich is a professional. A professional actress, a professional cameraman, a professional dress designer."[3] A clause in her contract stipulated that she could keep the fashions, negotiated at a 25 percent discount by Alfred Hitchcock. Another time, another couturier, another actress, same practice: in 1966, when Stanley Donen was making *Arabesque*, Sophia Loren asked to be outfitted by her friend Marc Bohan, Christian Dior's successor at the House of Dior: "Before she even began memorizing her lines, Loren stopped in Paris for costume fitting with Bohan and Roger Vivier (Dior's shoe designers, who would make the twenty-five pairs of shoes she wore in the film). All told, the Dior bill for the film weighed in at about $125,000, the equivalent of roughly one-quarter of Sophia's superstar salary. As per her standard arrangement, Sophia took the clothes home at the end of the production."[4]

"Christian Dior: French couturier born, in Granville in 1905. With the help of the industrialist Marcel Boussac, he founded the house that bears his name and, in February 1947, presented his first collection of haute couture as well as his first fragrance, Miss Dior, with which he copiously perfumed the salons of the runway shows." These few lines of information were supplied by a dictionary of proper names in the early 1950s. In 1956, the publication of the couturier's autobiography provided two hundred pages of anecdotes, thoughts, and analyses, sufficient to inundate this succinct portrait.

The question was not "Who is Dior?" but "What is Dior?" What is there beyond the proper name? What is the symbolic value of the word? In 1956, the filmmaker Norman Krasna shot *The Ambassador's Daughter*, with Olivia de Havilland in the title role. Naturally, the actress, a town client at the House of Dior, was dressed in Dior fashions in the film. The action takes place in Paris: a postcard Paris, an idyllic Paris for expatriate

OPPOSITE
In Henry Koster's *No Highway in the Sky* (1951), though Margaret Furse is mentioned in the credits as wardrobe supervisor, most of Marlene Dietrich's costumes were designed by Dior.

FOLLOWING PAGE
Poster for the film *No Highway in the Sky* (1951).

Americans. Olivia de Havilland, daughter of the United States ambassador, plays guide first to a senator's wife, then to a G.I. She leads them—that is, she leads viewers, foremost among them the American viewer—into that Paris of fantasies where all (or almost all) women are wearing Dior, and where even the little neighborhood bistro has a doorman, a maître d'hôtel, and Baccarat crystal on the tables. Gauguin and Monet, the Ritz and Place Vendôme, a brasserie with art nouveau decor, Notre-Dame, the Champs-Élysées, the Opéra Garnier: a cliché, Louis XIV Paris.

Here, of course, one drinks only champagne, one happens upon a procession of Bigoudens celebrating Fest Noz in the Eiffel Tower elevators, and one finds the means to tour all the cabarets in a single evening, from the Moulin Rouge to the Lido, even taking in a Bastille Day fireman's ball. A syncretic Paris, a magical city. "I like Paris. It's a sophisticated city," the G.I. muses. "This is Paris! I want to dance," proclaims the senator's wife. Sets, dialogue, costumes: everything is designed to inspire dreams. And in the mid-1950s, what inspired the most dreams in American women was haute couture. In that synecdochal Paris, where the exemplary possesses an absolute value (French art is summed up by impressionism, urban planning by the Paris of Baron Haussmann, the provinces by traditional folk costumes), fashion has only one name: Christian Dior. To say it aloud is to refer not only to the man who bears it but, more generally, to "haute couture"; it is to speak of luxury, to evoke the lady of Paris. In the American collective imagination, Dior is French culture. In the movie, that name is on everyone's lips. It brings a sparkle to the eye of the senator's wife, when she learns that her husband has just bought her a dress. It leads the ambassador, a general, and every noteworthy American in Paris to the Ritz for a runway show to benefit the Red Cross. That fashion show will appear again a little later in the film, on avenue Montaigne, where the camera lingers over the storefront of the boutique. More than a mere setting, the House of Dior also serves to advance the plot, since it is there that a series of mistaken identities sets the romantic comedy back in motion. Until the ambassador's daughter finally leaps into the arms of her handsome G.I. All dressed in Dior, of course: "This is Paris!"

Three years earlier, Howard Hawks had used the same plot device, but more succinctly, in *Gentlemen Prefer Blondes* (1953). Jane Russell and Marilyn Monroe, having just arrived in Paris, want to savor the joys of the capital. Jane Russell tells the taxi driver, "Pierre, we want to buy some clothes. You know? Hats, dresses . . . You know some good places?" The following shot pauses on a Dior storefront displaying the signature perfumes,

and two runway silhouettes are superimposed in the frame: a Bar suit for Marilyn Monroe and an evening gown for Jane Russell. The boutique is pure fantasy. The stone mascarons above the display windows suggest it is on Place Vendôme, where the House of Dior would not set up shop for the first time until November 2001. Even the logo affixed to the windows is fanciful. The printing is rounded, mannered, not quite of the era, whereas the original aspired to be resolutely modern. "Dior" appears by itself, with no first name—unimaginable in the couturier's time. That diminutive points to the house's fame across the Atlantic. In the eyes of American women, Christian Dior symbolized Paris couture and luxury, all the more glaringly for being elliptical.

Richard Sale followed up that first installment with a sequel, *Gentlemen Marry Brunettes* (1955). Now Jane Russell is accompanied by Jeanne Crain: two Broadway songsters, come to seek their fortunes in Paris, the "pleasure-loving city of the world," as the film trailer announces. Dior is an obligatory stop. Home shopping in this case, since it is in their hotel room that they receive a certain M. Mondeville, supposedly based on Christian Dior himself. "Souvenirs of Paris," the hotel manager offers, while bellhops enter, arms loaded down with Dior boxes: shoes, jewels, stockings, furs, as well as Miss Dior and Diorama, the first two signature perfumes. Renée and the other shop models of the time then present Cuba, Artamene, Moulin Rouge, and Mexico, the fashion designs of the Fall–Winter 1954 collection.

There are countless Hollywood films in which the proper name Dior (the man, his collections, his shop) is uttered. Real, fantasized, or a little of both, the name becomes a common noun in the American vocabulary, an antonomasia to express everything that is Paris couture.

1 "Le songe d'une nuit vénitienne," *L'Officiel de la couture de la mode de Paris*, with a photo essay by André Ostier and Heil, October 1951.
2 Christian Dior, *Christian Dior et moi*, (Paris: Librairie Amio-Dumont, 1956).
3 Quoted in Patrick McGilligan, *Alfred Hitchcock: A Life in Darkness and Light* (New York: HarperCollins Publishers, 2003).
4 Deirdre Donohue, *Sophia Style* (New York: Friedman/Fairfax, 2011).

Marlene Dietrich in *No Highway in the Sky* (1951) wears a design from a Christian Dior Haute Couture collection, around 1950.

INGRID BERGMAN
YVES MONTAND
ANTHONY PERKINS

IN THE *ANATOLE LITVAK* PRODUCTION

"GOODBYE AGAIN"

This is how love is... and always will be...

with **JESSIE ROYCE LANDIS** Screenplay by **SAMUEL TAYLOR**
Based upon the novel
"Aimez-Vous Brahms" by **FRANCOISE SAGAN** Produced and Directed by **ANATOLE LITVAK**

Released thru UNITED UA ARTISTS

OPPOSITE
Poster for the film *Goodbye Again* (1961).

ABOVE AND FOLLOWING TWO SPREADS
Ingrid Bergman and Anthony Perkins in Anatole Litvak's *Goodbye Again* (1961).

OPPOSITE
Poster for the film *Gentlemen Marry Brunettes* (1955).

ABOVE
A long letter sent to United Artists from the House of Dior stipulates: "It is understood that, for *Gentlemen Marry Brunettes*, you will call on us to present Parisian luxury and elegance *à la française*." It is in the hotel scene that this French-style luxury is particularly on display: the two actresses, Jane Russell and Jeanne Crain, with Dior packages and boxes piled on their laps, watch a private runway show from the House of Dior. Shop models Renée, Alla, Françoise, and Lison play themselves: they present the Moulin Rouge, Cuba, Artamene, and Mexico designs to the two heroines.

ABOVE
Olivia de Havilland in Norman Krasna's
Ambassador's Daughter (1956).

OPPOSITE
Poster for Norman Krasna's
Ambassador's Daughter (1956).

One of the sequences from *The Ambassador's Daughter* shows a runway show during which the Soirée Rose design is presented, Christian Dior Haute Couture collection, Fall–Winter 1955.

UNIVERSAL presents

MARLON BRANDO SOPHIA LOREN...

in

"A Countess from HONG KONG"

WRITTEN, DIRECTED and MUSIC by

CHARLES CHAPLIN

also starring

SYDNEY CHAPLIN and TIPPI HEDREN with PATRICK CARGILL

and MARGARET RUTHERFORD

PRODUCED by
JEROME EPSTEIN

TECHNICOLOR®

ABOVE
Sophia Loren in a special creation
by Marc Bohan for Christian Dior,
in Charlie Chaplin's *A Countess from
Hong Kong* (1967).

FOLLOWING SPREAD
Sophia Loren and Marlon Brando
during the shooting of *A Countess
from Hong Kong* (1967).

une manche et la Belle

présente par MICHEL SAFRA
avec MYLENE DEMONGEOT · HENRI VIDAL · ISA MIRANDA
dans une réalisation de HENRI VERNEUIL

d'après le roman de JAMES HADLEY CHASE
Adaptation de HENRI VERNEUIL · ANNETTE WADEMANT · FRANÇOIS BOYER
Dialogues de FRANÇOIS BOYER et ANNETTE WADEMANT

avec JEAN LOU PHILIPPE · SIMONE BACH · ANTONIN BERVAL · JEAN GALLAND · KY DUYEN · ANDRE ROANNE · MARC VALBEL
et ALFRED ADAM

Musique de Paul DURAND · Directeur Photographie Christian MATRAS · Décors J. A. d'AUBONNE
Directeur de la Production HENRI BAUM

SPVA FILMS

OPPOSITE
Seven-eighths-length Discrétion dress in Aleutian ivory, Christian Dior Haute Couture collection, Spring–Summer 1957. In a scene from Henri Verneuil's *Une manche et la belle*, Mylène Demongeot wears a customized Discrétion dress. The actress recalls:

"I had several fittings, which I found exceedingly boring! Since I was grumbling about having to stay on my feet for so long, the forewoman scolded me very severely, telling me: 'Young lady, Miss Dietrich can stand without moving for six hours!'"

ABOVE
Françoise Arnoul in Marcel Carné's
Le pays d'où je viens.

OPPOSITE
Poster for the film *Le pays d'où je viens*
(*The Country I Come From*; 1956).

150

C. L. M. CLÉMENT DUHOUR
Présente

GILBERT BÉCAUD

FRANÇOISE ARNOUL

dans un film de

MARCEL CARNÉ

LE PAYS D'OU JE VIENS

scénario de **J. EMMANUEL**

adaptation de MARCEL CARNÉ, MARCEL ACHARD et J. EMMANUEL

dialogues de **MARCEL ACHARD**
avec
MADELEINE LEBEAU
CLAUDE BRASSEUR et GABRIELLO

couleur par **TECHNICOLOR**

PAUL MARTY

Distribué par	directeur de la photographie	directeur de la production	ventes à l'étranger
COCINOR	PHILIPPE AGOSTINI	GILBERT BOKANOWSKI	MONDEX-FILMS

The trouble with house parties...is you
never can tell which parties will
end up playing house!

CARY GRANT | DEBORAH KERR | ROBERT MITCHUM | JEAN SIMMONS

THE GRASS IS GREENER

PROVES THAT VARIETY IS THE SPICE OF LOVE!!!

TECHNICOLOR® TECHNIRAMA

Produced and Directed by
STANLEY DONEN

Screenplay by HUGH and MARGARET WILLIAMS from their Great London Stage Success
A GRANDON PRODUCTION · A UNIVERSAL-INTERNATIONAL RELEASE

Music and lyrics by
NOEL COWARD
from his musical comedy hits!

OPPOSITE
Poster for the film *The Grass Is Greener* (1960).

ABOVE
Jean Simmons in Stanley Donen's *The Grass Is Greener* (1960), dressed in Christian Dior by Yves Saint Laurent.

153

Jean Simmons in a Christian Dior special creation by Yves Saint Laurent (around 1960), and Deborah Kerr dressed by Hardy Amies in *The Grass Is Greener* (1960).

IT'S SO EASY TO SET FIRE TO A

GINA LOLLOBRIGIDA
SEAN CONNERY
RALPH RICHARDSON

IN MICHAEL RELPH AND
BASIL DEARDEN'S PRODUCTION

...and between them was conceived murder

"WOMAN OF STRAW"

FROM THE NOVEL
BY CATHERINE ARLEY
DIRECTED BY
BASIL DEARDEN

ALSO STARRING
ALEXANDER KNOX
EASTMANCOLOR

SCREENPLAY BY
ROBERT MULLER
AND STANLEY MANN
RELEASED
THRU

PRODUCED BY
MICHAEL RELPH
UNITED ARTISTS

ABOVE
Gina Lollobrigida and Sean Connery
in Basil Dearden's *Woman of Straw.*

ABOVE
Mylène Demongeot in Michel Deville's
L'appartement des filles. She is wearing
a Christian Dior special creation by
Marc Bohan in cherry-print white cotton.

OPPOSITE
Poster from the film *L'appartement
des filles* (*Girl's Apartment*; 1963).

158

L'UNION GÉNÉRALE CINÉMATOGRAPHIQUE et les FILMS SIRIUS présentent

UNE PRODUCTION
PAUL GRAETZ

MYLENE DEMONGEOT
SYLVA KOSCINA
RENATE EWERT

AVEC
SAMI FREY

L'APPARTEMENT DES FILLES

D'APRÈS L'ŒUVRE DE
JACQUES ROBERT (Éditions René Julliard)
ADAPTATION DE
NINA COMPANEEZ et **MICHEL DEVILLE**
DIALOGUES DE
NINA COMPANEEZ

RÉALISATION DE
MICHEL DEVILLE AVEC
JEAN · FRANÇOIS CALVÉ ET
DANIEL CECCALDI

Dr. de PRODUCTION
JULIEN RIVIÈRE

Dr. de la PHOTOGRAPHIE
CLAUDE LECOMTE

MUSIQUE DE
JEAN DALVE

DISTRIBUTION

COPRODUCTION TRANSCONTINENTAL FILMS-Paris PRODUZIONI INTERCONTINENTALI-ROME CONSO FILMVERLEIH-MUNICH   VISA DE CENSURE 1019   IMP, SAINT-MARTIN, IMP, PARIS

ULTRA MOD **ULTRA MAD** **ULTRA MYSTERY**

GREGORY PECK

SOPHIA LOREN

A **STANLEY DONEN** PRODUCTION

ARABESQUE

TECHNICOLOR® **PANAVISION**®

with **ALAN BADEL** · KIERON MOORE

Screenplay by
JULIAN MITCHELL, STANLEY PRICE, PIERRE MARTON
Based on the novel "The Cipher" by GORDON COTLER

Music - **HENRY MANCINI**

Produced and Directed by **STANLEY DONEN** A UNIVERSAL RELEASE

2040

OPPOSITE
Poster from the Stanley Donen
film *Arabesque* (1966).

ABOVE
In Stanley Donen's *Arabesque*, Marc Bohan for Christian Dior designed the special creations worn by Sophia Loren, while Roger Vivier for Christian Dior designed her shoes. As in *Charade*, the director stages a detective story as elegant as it is extravagant, as attested by Sophia Loren's outfits: a transparent striped evening gown over toile de Jouy background pattern, a gold lamé dress with Oriental hood, and an emerald green wool coat accented with a small panther hat—not to mention the multicolor feather mule slippers or white vinyl thigh-high boots.

ABOVE
Sophia Loren in *Arabesque*, wearing a
special creation of Indian (or Maharaja)
inspiration.

OPPOSITE
Sophia Loren in a fuchsia and deep purple
shantung suit printed with chevron motifs
by Sachë, a variation on the Fifth Avenue
design, Christian Dior collection by
Marc Bohan, Spring–Summer 1965.

151

PIERRE O'CONNELL et ARYS NISSOTTI présentent

Un film de
JULIEN DUVIVIER
BRIGITTE AUBER
JEAN BROCHARD
RENÉ BLANCARD
PAUL FRANKEUR
RAYMOND HERMANTIER
DANIEL IVERNEL
PIERRE DESTAILLES
CHRISTIANE LENIER
MARIE-FRANCE

ARNSTAM

Sous le Ciel de Paris

Scénario original de JULIEN DUVIVIER - Adaptation de RENÉ LEFÈVRE et JULIEN DUVIVIER
Dialogues de RENÉ LEFÈVRE - Commentaire de HENRI JEANSON dit par FRANÇOIS PÉRIER
avec MARCELLE PRAINCE et SYLVIE

Directeur de Production : LOUIS DE MASURE

Distribué par
Filmsonor

PRODUCTION
REGINA
Filmsonor

BEDOS & Cie IMPRIMEURS PARIS

OPPOSITE
Poster for the film *Sous le ciel de Paris*
(*Under the Paris Sky*; 1951).

ABOVE
Scene from the Julien Duvivier film
Sous le ciel de Paris, featuring designs
from the Christian Dior Haute Couture
collection, Fall–Winter 1950. From
left to right: the Romanesque dance
dress and bolero jacket, the Périchole
dance dress, the Rigodon dance dress,
the Europe grand gala dress, and the
Océanie gala dress.

ABOVE
Brigitte Bardot in Michel Deville's
L'Ours et la Poupée, wearing a Christian
Dior special creation by Marc Bohan.

OPPOSITE
Poster from the film *L'Ours et la
Poupée* (*The Bear and the Doll*; 1970).

A Starring Role for the Costume

It was unusual for Christian Dior, personally, and the House of Dior more generally, to design costumes especially for a film. In the vast majority of cases, the clothes in the collections seen onscreen were chosen by the actresses, as they would have done in their personal shopping. They are altered—there is no haute couture without customizing—but still literal. They therefore tell us something about the relationships among the characters, especially from a social perspective. In Alfred Hitchcock's *Stage Fright* (1950), for example, Marlene Dietrich, dressed head-to-toe in Dior, plays the role of a star, both actress and singer, while Jane Wyman, a student at a drama school, wears a simple blouse and a little cardigan sweater. Wyman is told by Michael Wilding, "Oh, you don't look like an actress." Later in the film, when she is more directly propelling the plot, her appearance has become somewhat more sophisticated, even "Diorized," but without being Dior (the pleats in her long skirt give a fleeting glimpse of a generous length of fabric, and the bow around her neck has polka dots, both major features of the couturier's work). Wilder then says, "You'll make a very good actress indeed." In the movies, Alfred Hitchcock seems to be telling us, clothes make the actress. And Dior makes the star.

That same idea of the diegetic costume can also be found in Roy Baker's *Don't Bother to Knock* (1952). In one scene, Marilyn Monroe, a young woman with a troubled past, having become a babysitter, compliments Lurene Tuttle (the mother of the child Marilyn is watching) on her evening gown, while Marilyn herself is wearing a simple shirtdress. Here clothes take on an aspirational dimension, their symbolic power becoming an object of fascination. In a later scene, caught red-handed wearing her boss's things (dressed, made-up, bejeweled), Marilyn will offer this excuse: "I just wanted to see how they looked on me." In addition to the light these two scenes shed on social relationships, a comparison between the two can tell us something about the schizophrenic dimension of the character played by Marilyn.

Costumes sometimes play an even greater role, becoming part of the plot in the same capacity as a character. In Mark Robson's *The Little Hut* (1957), Ava Gardner is dressed entirely in Dior, with no fewer than fourteen outfits. In the opening credits, "Christian Dior of Paris" takes up the whole screen; the couturier's name appears in even larger letters than that of the director of photography. The opening shot shows a screen. A hand, presumed to be that of Ava Gardner, places a dress over it, then a pair of stockings. The character remains hidden behind the screen, symbolized solely by her clothing. Same thing with a man's hand and a Stetson. Then a bowler hat, set down by another man's hand. Like a film synopsis, that opening sequence presents the plot: Ava Gardner is caught between two men, Stewart Granger (assumed to be the man in the Stetson) and David Niven (no doubt represented by the derby). Furthermore, that little sketch, by placing clothing at the center of the action, announces the importance it will later assume in the film. The three companions are washed up on a desert island after Stewart Granger's yacht is shipwrecked. Having been caught by the storm during dinner, the two men are wearing suits and Ava Gardner is in an evening gown. They will have no changes of clothing for their long weeks of isolation. No matter! With her one outfit, Ava will put together something to wear for every occasion. Her shawl will become a sari, her slip will double as a swimsuit, and she will wear her necklace sometimes around her neck, sometimes in her hair. The only other accessory she will have is a wicker hat woven out of palm leaves. The dialogue also lends support to the theme. For example, Ava Gardner, Stewart Granger's onscreen wife, will cite as grounds for divorce the lack of attention he pays to her clothes: "After he'd been away for weeks, his very first night home, he went straight to bed . . . and never even noticed my divine new nightie . . . I bet you can't even tell me what color it was." And the husband, very saddened, wryly acknowledges, "Respondent admits inability to recall hue of sleepwear." Divorce is almost a foregone conclusion. But then Stewart Granger takes back his confession: "Something I suddenly remember . . . that night I came home from New York, the color of your nightie was pale yellow, and your negligee was white with green frills." Divorce is now out of the question!

Ava Gardner and David Niven
in *The Little Hut*.

GAUMONT-DISTRIBUTION présente un film de MELVILLE-PRODUCTIONS

Une réalisation de
JEAN PIERRE MELVILLE

les Enfants Terribles

D'après le roman célèbre de
JEAN COCTEAU

NICOLE STÉPHANE · ÉDOUARD DERMITHE
avec
RENÉE COSIMA · JACQUES BERNARD
MEL MARTIN · MARIA CYLIAKUS · JEAN MARIE ROBAIN
MAURICE REVEL · ADELINE AUGOC · RACHEL DEVYRIS
et
ROGER GAILLARD

Gaumont-Distribution 40. Champs-Elysées. Paris. Bal. 44.04

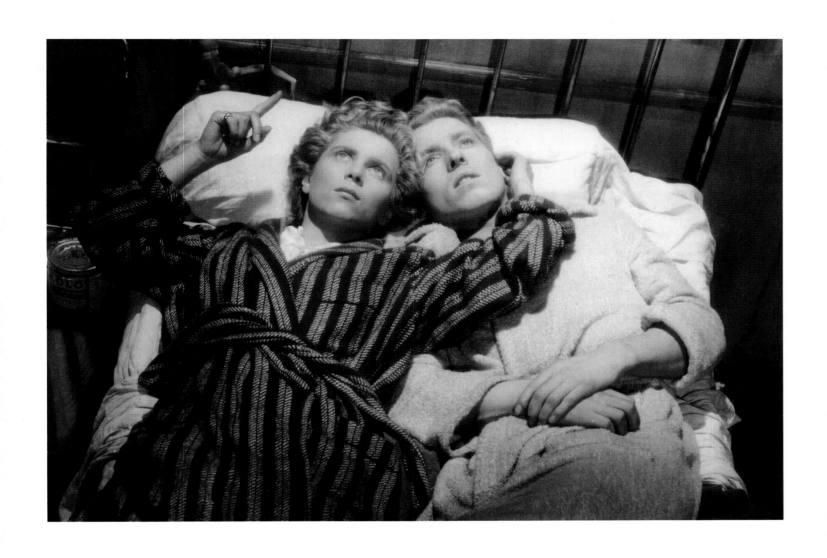

OPPOSITE
Poster for the film *Les Enfants terribles*
(*The Terrible Children*; 1950).

ABOVE
Nicole Stéphane and Edouard Dermithe
in Jean-Pierre Melville's *Les Enfants
terribles*. The terrycloth bathrobe will
create a lasting impression; the magazine
L'Express will even call the film a "tragedy
in terrycloth bathrobe" (April 7, 1975).

"You walk right up to the client from a long way off, hands on your hips, thumbs thrust forward, looking into her eyes as if you were picking a quarrel with her." That is the advice received by the apprentice Dior model Nicole Stéphane (above) in the film *Les Enfants terribles*, written by Jean Cocteau and directed by Jean-Pierre Melville.

JANE WYMAN · MARLENE DIETRICH
MICHAEL WILDING · RICHARD TODD

DANS LE FILM DE

ALFRED HITCHCOCK

LE GRAND ALIBI

ALISTAIR SIM · DAME SYBIL THORNDIKE
SCÉNARIO DE WHITFIELD COOK
ADAPTATION D'ALMA REVILLE
DIALOGUE ADDITIONNEL DE JAMES BRIDIE
D'APRÈS LE ROMAN DE SELWYN JEPSON

ABOVE
In Alfred Hitchcock's *Stage Fright*, Marlene Dietrich imposes her friend and couturier Christian Dior: "No Dior, no Dietrich!" Hitchcock, well known for the care he takes in developing his heroines' style, will have to give in to the star's demands. Her contract requires a Dior wardrobe (which she was allowed to keep after the end of shooting). With no hard feelings, the director will admit: "Miss Dietrich is a professional. A professional actress, a professional cameraman, a professional dress designer!"

Marlene Dietrich and Alfred Hitchcock
during the shooting of *Stage Fright*
(1950).

Marlene Dietrich in *Stage Fright*, in an
Acacia suit, Christian Dior Haute Couture
collection, Spring–Summer 1949.

OPPOSITE
Marlene Dietrich in a special
creation for *Stage Fright*.

ABOVE
Marlene Dietrich in a Grande Saison
short evening gown in pale pink organza
embroidered in pink, Christian Dior
Haute Couture collection, Spring–
Summer 1949.

Marlene Dietrich in the Palais
Rose design, mother-of-pearl
mousse embroidery, Christian Dior
Haute Couture collection,
Spring–Summer 1949.

DIOR & HIS FILMS

"Fashion is a theater." That metaphor, proposed by Christian Dior, is spun out from collection to collection and passed down from designer to designer. The runway shows—scripted, staged, and produced as epic films—weave the narrative of a saga that began in 1947. That theatrical scene continues onscreen, in commercials for fragrances, and especially, the latest opus for J'Adore, filmed by Jean-Jacques Annaud, in which Christian Dior pays tribute to the actresses—for they too made Dior history.

All the World's a Stage

The imposing building at 30, avenue Montaigne, is a theater. On fashion show days, the staircases are tiers of seats, where the viewers of the great spectacle take their places. The play being performed is called *Corolle, En 8, Y,* or *Trapèze*. Fashion models are the actresses, and the characters they play bear the names of the designs: Batignolles, Exotique, Gitane, Soirée de Réveillon. The show is in "Odorama" : since 1947, Miss Dior has perfumed the salon during performances.

That comparison comes from Christian Dior himself, and he spins out the metaphor for the length of his autobiography, imagining he is an actor in the great theater of fashion: "After that, I had to dedicate myself to the role of Christian Dior, couturier; a role that in that bright season I was learning in Paris, before the hour of doom when I would take it on the road. . . . They were expecting Antinous, Petronius, a pinup boy, something consistent with the image of the couturier as depicted in the movies or the theater."[1] He made designs like a dramatist, built his collections like a director. "A couturier preparing to put on a two-hour show—with no plot and no intermission—has worries unknown to the director," he writes.[2]

Screen adaptations of the runway shows would come later. They can undoubtedly be traced back to the time of Christian Dior himself, since the extreme coherence of his collections, structured around a new silhouette every season, were able to serve as a guiding thread, if not as a synopsis. It was primarily in the late 1990s and early 2000s, however, that Dior fashion shows became more clearly centered around themes, becoming true narratives. Narration, set, lighting, body language of the model-actresses: everything in these runway-shows-turned-tableaux-vivants attracts the spectator's attention to the gown-costumes, as exaggerated the acting in a silent film. *Poetic Homage to the Marchesa Casati* was the title of the haute couture runway show of Spring–Summer 1998, which had the structure of a six-act play, plus prologue: act 2 was titled, "Story in an English Garden"; act 4, "Lascivious Story to a Tango Beat."

In 2005, Christian Dior would have been a hundred years old. The haute couture runway show of that Fall–Winter was therefore conceived as the film of the couturier's life: Little by little, the light comes up on the catwalk, like a fade-in for an opening scene. The stage reveals the main gate to a villa, called Les Rhumbs. It is there that the Dior family lives, in Granville, Normandy. It is early morning. The sky is dark and ominous, lightning flashes across it. Ivy runs along the wrought iron of the entry gate and the length of the stone decorations, evoking the lush vegetation of the original garden passionately maintained by Christian Dior and his mother. A thick mist renders the outlines of the set evanescent, somewhat like Italian *sfumato* of the fifteenth and sixteenth centuries. The atmosphere is that of a fantasy film. A horse-drawn carriage enters the frame. The little boy who emerges is certainly Christian Dior, in a sailor suit, short pants, knee socks, and round hat. The time is prior to World War I, and he is not yet ten. His mother follows. She is his first model, his first inspiration: the very picture of the *grande bourgeoise* whom the couturier always dreamed of dressing. In fact, his first fashion line will be named Madeleine, after Madame Dior.

Our young Christian—his intimates call him "Tian"—sits at the front of the catwalk and watches the characters go by, embodying the many powerful images that will subsequently influence his style and work. The first tableau could therefore be called "the formative years." Nearly half a century later, these Belle Époque women with their well-defined waistlines, their bustles, their aristocratic bearing, and their long gowns will inspire the New Look. The second tableau immerses us in the early years of the House of Dior: "I wanted to be an architect. Being a couturier, I am obliged to follow architectural laws and principles." Dior's words, quoted in voiceover, function as an inter-title in sound, bringing to mind the title cards in silent films but also the abrupt cuts of New Wave cinema, especially the films of Jean-Luc Godard, Jacques Demy, and Éric Rohmer. They introduce a new chapter while announcing its content.

Other quotations from the couturier and excerpts from press articles of the late 1940s and early 1950s punctuate the transitions. They are like little *explications de texte* of the fashions, and they also set the scene for the runway show: the soundtrack, the breathing, the crackling, the entire sound atmosphere evoking the old radios of the time. A sequence on the eighteenth century—Christian Dior's favorite era—follows, another inspired by Venice and its masked balls, a third on Hollywood stars (the designs are called Vivien, Marlène, Ginger, Ava, Rita). All the couturier's major themes are staged like a play. Then, at the end of the show, the character of the young Christian returns, as if he were contemplating his life parading by haute couture unfolding before his eyes.

These runway shows, scripted like epic films, also borrow their principles of production: a powerful opening scene (the first fashion design is always very strong stylistically) and a grand finale. Every season, a page of acknowledgments is distributed to the guests, functioning exactly like film credits, listing set direction, lighting, music, hair styling, makeup, staging, production: the work done behind the scenes.

Let us pause for a moment on makeup. Rouge Dior, the house's first lipstick, arrived on the display counters in 1949.

ABOVE
Lauren Bacall and Humphrey Bogart
in the front row of a Dior runway show
in 1952. Photograph by Willy Maywald.

FOLLOWING PAGE
As a major client for the House of
Dior, Sophia Loren regularly attended
the runway shows (as here in 1968).
Photograph by Raymond Depardon.

199

It was joined in 1958 by a face powder. The first complete line of makeup dates to 1969. Today the models always wear Dior makeup for the runway shows. Backstage, the fitting rooms could be mistaken for movie dressing rooms: the same hair stylists, the same lighted mirrors. From the audience's vantage point, the site is just as spectacular: facial features are exaggerated, expressions invented. You would think you were watching a Japanese Noh play, traditional Chinese theater, or a German Expressionist film. Makeup becomes a magnifying mask, just as the clothes selected for the runway are a sort of archetype of the collection.

Cinema and makeup are so intimately linked that, in 1974, a dedicated line of products came into being, launched at the impetus of the Soviet Mosfilm studios: Visiora. Its packaging used the motif of a piece of film, and the makeup had a range of colors adapted for a certain high-speed Kodak film stock, used by Russian filmmakers of the time: a matte lipstick, so as not to reflect the spotlights; a rain-resistant fixative; bleaching agents for the hair. The success of the Visiora line would extend well beyond the borders of the Soviet Union, and new gray and white packaging—more chic, more Dior—would accompany its development. "Maquillage Cinéma-Télévision," it was called. And actors such as Claudine Auger, Claudia Cardinale, and Marcelo Mastroianni would not hesitate to wear the makeup around town as well, adopting it for their personal use.

"Dior continues to be the center of attraction for famous visitors. Every afternoon, his salon becomes a true diorama featuring the most illustrious names of high society and of the whole world." So wrote Elstir, a society columnist for the magazine *L'Officiel de la couture et de la mode de Paris* in December 1949. He went on to list the elegant ladies of the time, Dior addicts from day one: diplomat's wives, daughters of important families, wives of industrialists. The names have long since been forgotten. In the late 1940s, however, they were no less familiar to readers than "Greta Garbo, who appeared without dark glasses, and smiling," or Marlene Dietrich, "next to the Princess of Réthy." The American stars who attended the runway shows were clients like the rest, and no less stars for all that. In any case, there was no everywoman at the Dior show. The women smoked, entertained themselves, engaged in small talk. And when the models paraded among them, the salons at the mansion on 30, avenue Montaigne, were so packed that the voluminous gowns seemed to have trouble making their way through.

All the women were dressed in Dior. Both models and clients—who in a sense became models themselves. But the crowd's attention focused on the models: they were the ones wearing the new fashions. The actresses, usually the center of attention, became mere spectators. Olivia de Havilland was already an Oscar winner, Rita Hayworth had already turned heads the world over by singing "Put the Blame on Mame" in *Gilda*, and Marlene Dietrich had already been for some time the blonde angel of film. Nevertheless, in the haute couture salons, the real actresses were named Tania, Lucile, Alla, Marie-Thérèse, Paule, and later, Victoire. These were the couturier's shop models, and during runway shows it was they who were the stars dressed in Dior.

The evolution of the model into an actress and the actress into a spectator continued over time, reaching its climax with the publicity for the fragrance J'adore. In the commercial, Charlize Theron plays a top model opening a Dior fashion show. Backstage, fiction and reality merge: through the magic of cinema and special effects, she runs into Grace Kelly, Marlene Dietrich, and Marilyn Monroe, who have also become runway models, as well as Morgane Dubled and Thana Kuhnen, real-life models and now actresses in the commercial, where they play the role of—models! Continuing the confusion: although the three Hollywood myths are models in the script as it unfolds, they remain actresses in the shots in which they appear. Marlene Dietrich, for example, reprises her character Lola Lola from *Der blaue Engel* (*The Blue Angel*; 1930): same attitude, same performance. Same character in sum. And yet her light-colored hat is now black, and a Bar suit jacket covers her shoulders, which are bare in the Joseph von Sternberg film. Even the cut of her hair is slightly different. With that makeover, is she not an actress playing a model, breathing new life into the actress playing the model? Same thing with Marilyn Monroe: the straps on her dress recall the one she wore in *The Seven Year Itch* (1955). As for Grace Kelly, her hieratic dress, pose, and face seem to come right out of *To Catch a Thief* (1955).

[1] Christian Dior, *Christian Dior et moi* (Paris: Librairie Amio-Dumont, 1956) .
[2] *Ibid.*

ABOVE
Rita Hayworth during a Dior
runway show in 1956.

OPPOSITE
Marlene Dietrich during
a Dior runway show in 1951.
Photographie Willy Maywald.

Ginger dress in shaded yellow tulle embroidered with turquoise, worn with a trompe l'oeil flesh-colored corset (left); Marlène dress in shaded blue tulle with multicolor embroidery, worn with a trompe l'oeil flesh-colored corset (middle); Vivien dress in shaded crimson tulle embroidered with gold and turquoise, worn with a trompe l'oeil flesh-colored corset (right). Christian Dior Haute Couture collection by John Galliano, Fall–Winter 2005.

ABOVE
Eva Herzigova, photographed by
Paolo Roversi, in the Vivien dress,
Christian Dior Haute Couture
collection by John Galliano,
Fall–Winter 2005.

OPPOSITE
Vivien dress in shaded crimson tulle
embroidered with gold and turquoise,
worn with a trompe l'oeil flesh-colored
corset. Christian Dior Haute Couture
collection by John Galliano,
Fall–Winter 2005.

ABOVE
Kirsty Hume, photographed by
Paolo Roversi, in the Marlène dress,
Christian Dior Haute Couture
collection by John Galliano,
Fall–Winter 2005.

OPPOSITE
Shalom Harlow, photographed by
Paolo Roversi, in the Ginger dress,
Christian Dior Haute Couture
collection by John Galliano,
Fall–Winter 2005.

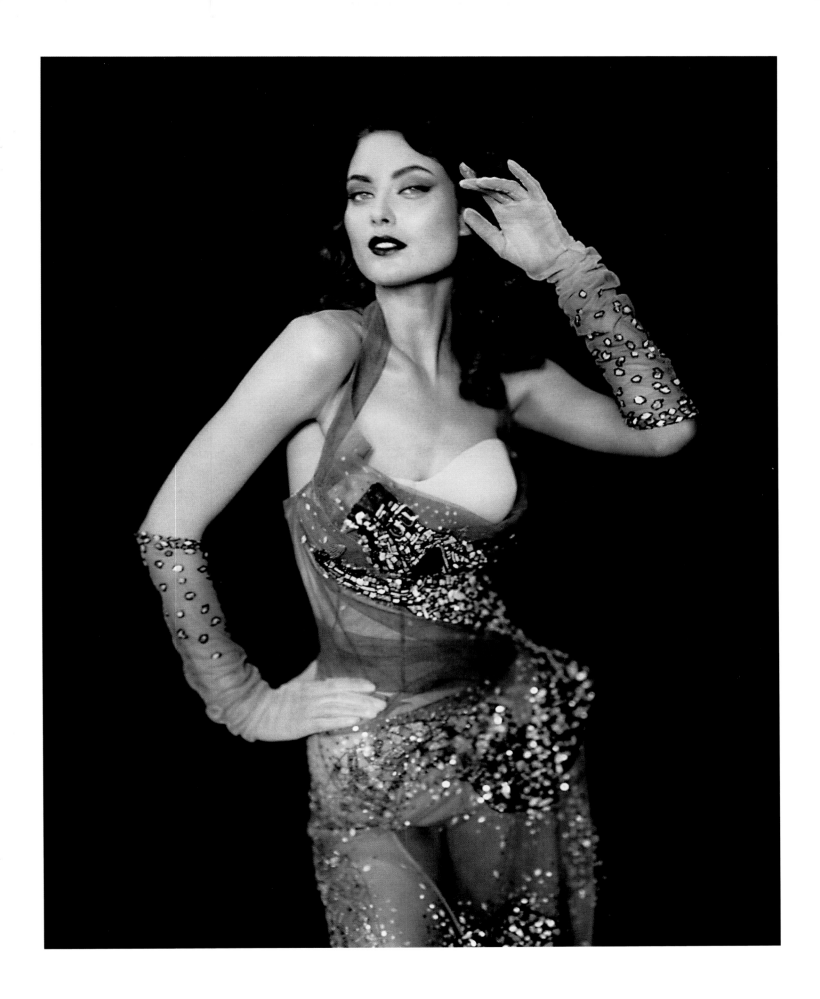

Synopsis

Behind its main wrought-iron gate, the Château de Versailles. The façade is illuminated, night has fallen, the gate is locked, with everything that implies in terms of exclusivity. A private Versailles, a personal visit. It is here that French taste was constructed, luxury defined, culture perfected. On the stone steps of a monumental staircase, the clicking of heels. Were it not for the blonde hair, picked up by the gold in the ironwork of the banisters, the dark silhouette could belong to Belphégor, the phantom of the Louvre played by Juliette Gréco on 1960s television. Fitted jeans, Bar jacket. In the Galerie des Glaces, the light of the chandeliers reflects its colors ad infinitum; the marble glows red, contrasting with the characters' black dress code. Here an haute couture runway show will take place; and, at the sight of our heroine heading backstage, passing the wall of photographers and the rows of chairs where the guests await, there can be no doubt she will be part of it. Behind the scenes, where everyone is waiting for her, she hands off her bag—a Lady Dior—and her dark glasses to her assistants. It's Charlize Theron.

In this short film, she plays the part of a fashion model and rejoins the other runway girls backstage. In the first place, that Hollywood beauty, seen from the back, wearing a grand evening gown—we recognize the Dior Prêt-à-porter collection from Fall 2010. And that man, kneeling in front of the woman with the graceful gestures, adjusting the bow on her dress, isn't that Christian Dior himself? The two models kiss as if they have known each other forever. The unidentified woman turns around: it's Grace, princess of Monaco, née Kelly from the era of Cinemascope. Grace 1955, Charlize 2011. Dior Haute Couture Spring-Summer 1997 and Christian Dior 1947. The camera comes in close. We feel the urgency, the imminence of the runway show. The fashion models get ready, making the last adjustments: a corset laced, eyelash liner applied, cleavage powdered, underskirt zipped up. Charlize takes off her jacket. She is presented with the dress she will wear on the catwalk, all in gold and flesh tones. Her Maasai-style necklace stands out against her bare shoulders, recalling the neck of the J'adore bottle. Farther away, in front of her dressing table, amid the Dior boxes and the flashes of the photographers' cameras, is Marlene Dietrich, her legs going on forever, her pumps and the arch of her foot, the curve of her hips and the line of her stockings high up on her thighs. Marlene, femme fatale, in a Bar jacket from the Fall-Winter 2007 Haute Couture collection. Marlene 1930 patterned on Lola Lola from *Der Blaue Engel*. Marlene the temptress, Marlene the forbidden fruit, provocative Marlene. A little Carmen as well, seeming to express with her eyes: "If you don't love me, I love you. If I love you, watch out!"

The music in the commercial resumes its pounding rhythm, then marks a pause in its crescendo, as if to prepare for its finale. Charlize is about to make her entrance. There it is, that embroidered skirt, worn with a flesh-colored corset. That mauve jacket, that canary suit. The wedding dress flies up as she hurries past. Surrounded in a halo of light from the bulbs around her mirror, Marilyn Monroe is applying red lipstick. Her dress recalls the one she wore in *The Seven Year Itch*; she points to the bottle on her dressing table. Charlize finishes: "J'adore." Marilyn takes the perfume in her hands. The Galerie des Glaces goes dark. Backstage, the fashion models are lined up in the order they will appear on the catwalk. Charlize will open the show; rushing, she goes to the head of the line, the way one would go back in time. In the background, we discover the entire collection and the fashion models who are wearing it: the Dior fitting room, with Grace, Marilyn, and Marlene ready to walk the runway after her. The music erupts as Charlize makes her entrance. And the perfume bottle—its design reminiscent of the curves of the *En 8* line, which Christian Dior presented in 1947 for his first haute couture collection—is superimposed over the image, placed over her silhouette, to underscore all that is feminine about it. Symbolic connections defying chronology. Dior makes his movie, retracing the history of Hollywood glamour through its iconic stars, reappropriating for himself the ones who had appropriated him, at the height of glory, around town or onscreen.

Charlize Theron, photographed
by Jean-Baptiste Mondino
for J'adore, 2006.

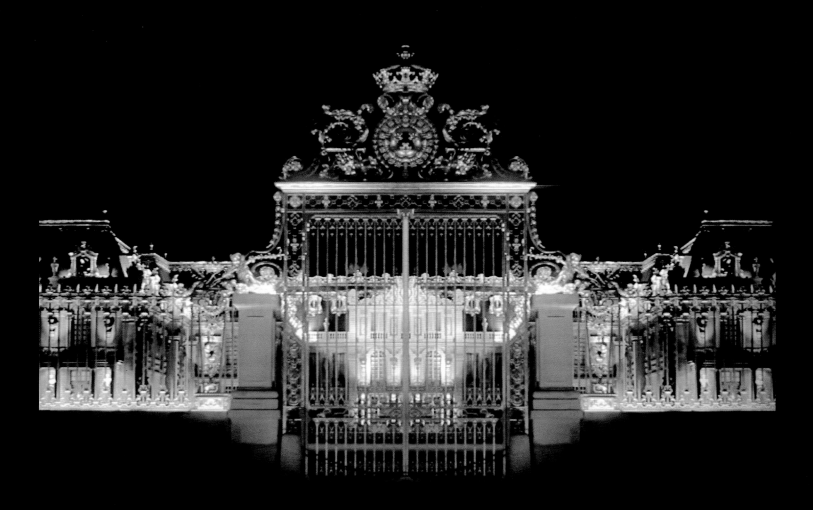

J'adore

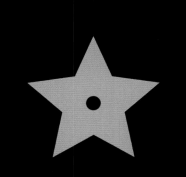

Filmography

Yves Saint Laurent for Christian Dior

1958   *Indiscreet*, Stanley Donen (Ingrid Bergman)

1958   *Les Tricheurs* (*The Cheaters*), Marcel Carné
(Pascale Petit, Andréa Parisy)

1959   *Libel*, Anthony Asquith (Olivia de Havilland)

1959   *La fièvre monte à El Pao*, Luis Buñuel (María Félix)

1960   *The Grass Is Greener*, Stanley Donen (Jean Simmons)

1960   *Les Collants noirs* (*Black Tights*), Terence Young

1960   *La estrella vacía*, Emilio Gómez Muriel (María Félix)

1960   *À bout de souffle* (*Breathless*), Jean-Luc Godard

Marc Bohan for Christian Dior

1961   *Goodbye Again*, Anatole Litvak (Ingrid Bergman)

1961   *Don't Bother to Knock*, Cyril Frankel (Nicole Maurey)

1961   *Phaedra*, Jules Dassin (Melina Mercouri)

1961   *A Gift of Time* (television series), Garcin Kamin
(Olivia de Havilland)

1962   *Light in the Piazza*, Guy Green (Olivia de Havilland)

1963   *L'Appartement des filles* (*Girl's Apartment*), Michel Deville
(Mylène Demongeot and Sylva Koscina)

1963   *A New Kind of Love*, Melville Shavelson (Joanne Woodward)

1963   *Topkapi*, Jules Dassin (Melina Mercouri)

1964   *Woman of Straw*, Basil Dearden (Gina Lollobrigida)

1964   *The Beauty Jungle*, Val Guest (Janette Scott for evening wear)

1964   *Paris When It Sizzles*, Richard Quine (Marlene Dietrich)

1966   *Arabesque*, Stanley Donen (Sophia Loren);
BAFTA nomination for Best Costume

1967   *A Countess from Hong Kong*, Charlie Chaplin
(Sophia Loren)

1967   *The Double Man*, Franklin J. Schaffner (Moira Lister)

1968   *Secret Ceremony*, Joseph Losey (Elizabeth Taylor)

1970   *L'ours et la poupée* (*The Bear and the Doll*), Michel Deville
(Brigitte Bardot)

1970   *The Lady in the Car with Glasses and Gun*, Anatole Litvak
(Samantha Eggar and Stéphane Audran)

1970   *Un beau monstre* (*Love Me Strangely*), Sergio Gobbi
(Virna Lisi)

1973   *Rude journée pour la reine*, René Allio (Simone Signoret)

1974   *Ironie du Sort* (*The Irony of Chance*), Edouard Molinaro
(Marie-Hélène Breillat)

1974   *La Race des seigneurs* (*Creezy*), Pierre Granier-Deferre
(Sydne Rome)

1974   *Les Seins de glace* (*Someone is Bleeding*), Georges Lautner
(Mireille Darc)

1974   *Verdict*, André Cayatte (Sophia Loren)

1975   *L'Agression* (*Act of Aggression*), Gérard Pirès

1975   *Le Chat et la Souris* (*Cat and Mouse*), Claude Lelouch
(Michèle Morgan)

1976   *The Cassandra Crossing*, George P. Cosmatos (Sophia Loren)

1977   *L'homme qui aimait les femmes* (*The Man Who Loved Women*),
François Truffaut

1978   *Le Dernier Amant romantique* (*The Last Romantic Lover*),
Just Jaeckin (Dayle Haddon)

1981   *Tout feu, tout flamme* (*All Fired Up*), Jean-Paul Rappeneau
(Isabelle Adjani and Lauren Hutton)

1983   *The Moon in the Gutter*, Jean-Jacques Beneix
(Nastassja Kinski)

1985   *Bras de fer*, Gérard Vergez (Ángela Molina, Bernard Giraudeau,
Christophe Malavoy); Costumes from the 1940s created
from original and previously unseen designs by Christian Dior;
nominated for César Award for Best Costume Design.

1986   *Conseil de famille*, Costa-Gavras (Fanny Ardant)

1986   *Corps et biens* (*With All Hands*), Benoît Jacquot
(Dominique Sanda)

1986   *La Femme de ma vie* (*The Woman of My Life*), Régis Wargnier

1988   *Bonjour l'angoisse*, Pierre Tchernia (Pierre Arditi dressed in Dior)

1988   *Trois places pour le 26* (*Three Seats for the 26th*), Jacques Demy

Gianfranco Ferré for Christian Dior

1990   *Corps perdus*, Eduardo de Gregorio

1994   *L'Ange noir*, Jean-Claude Brisseau (Sylvie Vartan)

1994   *Grosse Fatigue* (*Dead Tired*), (Michel Blanc dressed by
Patrick Lavoix for Christian Dior Monsieur)

1994   *Prêt-à-porter*, Robert Altman (Sophia Loren)

1994   *La Malaimée*, Jean-Paul Scarpitta

1995   *Les Cent et Une Nuits de Simon Cinéma*, Agnès Varda

1996   *Madame Verdoux*, Jean-Luc Raynaud

John Galliano for Christian Dior

2000   *Dr. T and the Women*, Robert Altman (Helen Hunt,
Farrah Fawcett, Kate Hudson, Liv Tyler, almost all the
women patients dressed in Dior)

2001   *Mistinguett, la dernière revue*, Jérôme Savary
(Liliane Montevecchi, Jean-Marc Thibault, and
Ginette Garcin, scene filmed in the boutique)

2001   *Legally Blonde*, Robert Luketic (Ali Larter)

2002   *Spider-Man*, Sam Raimi (Kirsten Dunst)

2004   *La confiance règne* (*Confidence Reigns*), Etienne Chatillez
(Vincent Lindon, Cécile de France, scene filmed in front
of the boutique at 30, avenue Montaigne, Cécile de France
dressed in Dior)

2004   *Les Parisiens* (*The Parisians*), Claude Lelouch (Maïwenn)

2004   *Les gens honnêtes vivent en France*, Bob Decout (Victoria Abril)

2004   *People Jet Set 2*, Fabien Onteniente (Ornella Muti)

2005   *Backstage*, Emmanuelle Bercot (Emmanuelle Seigner)

2009   *Los abrazos rotos* (*Broken Embraces*), Pedro Almodóvar
(Penélope Cruz)

2009   *Coco*, Gad Elmaleh (Pascale Arbillot)

2011   *Midnight in Paris*, Woody Allen (Rachel McAdams)

2011   *Bridesmaids*, Paul Feig (Kristen Wiig, Maya Rudolph)

Index

Acknowledgments

The project was made possible thanks to support from Bernard Arnault, Sidney Toledano and Claude Martinez.

We would like to thank Frederic Auerbach, Kate Barry, Patrick Demarchelier, Elliott Erwitt, Laziz Hamani, Peter Lindbergh, Alexi Lubomirski, Nick Knight, Craig McDean, Jean-Baptiste Mondino, Willy Rizzo, Paolo Roversi, Philippe Schlienger, Emanuele Scorcelletti, Mark Shaw, Mario Sorrenti, Bert Stern, Nicolas Tikhomiroff, and Jan Welters.

Isabelle Adjani, Françoise Arnoul, Lauren Bacall, Brigitte Bardot, Drew Barrymore, Monica Bellucci, Laëtitia Casta, Marion Cotillard, Penélope Cruz, Olivia de Havilland, Mylène Demongeot, Jennifer Garner, Eva Green, Anne Hathaway, Lauren Hutton, Nicole Kidman, Mélanie Laurent, Gina Lollobrigida, Sophia Loren, Eva Mendès, Carey Mulligan, Kim Novak, Sarah Jessica Parker, Natalie Portman, Sharon Stone, Tilda Swinton, Charlize Theron, and Reese Witherspoon.

Oneta Jackson (Patrick Demarchelier Studio), Carlo Giusti Productions, Alexandre Lamare (Management Artists), Sandra Laupa (Iconothèque de la Cinémathèque Française), Lisa Lavender (Bert Stern), Jutta Niemann (Association Willy Maywald), Dominique Rizzo, Hervé Szerman, and Tiziana Trischitta.

Special thanks to Olivier Bialobos, Jean-Paul Claverie and Jérôme Pulis.

Christian Dior Couture
Solène Auréal, Olivier Bialobos, Cécile Chamouard-Aykanat, Fanni Bakos, Gérald Chevalier, Jérôme Gautier, Jérôme Hanover, Stacey Kubasak, Philippe Le Moult, Charlotte Martin, Soizic Pfaff, and Perrine Scherrer.

Christian Dior Parfums
Frédéric Bourdelier, Sandrine Boury-Heyler, Vincent Leret, Jérôme Pulis, and Jessica Robert.

LVMH / Moët Hennessy. Louis Vuitton
Jean-Paul Claverie and Loïc Bégard.

The Musée Christian Dior wishes to thank the Cinémathèque Française and, in particular, Serge Toubiana, Charlyne Carrère, Catherine Lemerige, Jacques Ayroles; the Cinémathèque de Berlin and, in particular, Silke Ronneburg, Barbara Shroeter, Werner Sudendorf, Herrn Werner; Louis Vuitton Malletier, Direction du Patrimoine, and, in particular, Antoine Jarrier, Raphaël Gérard, Eva Rica and Marie Wurry; Didier Ludot, François Hurteau-Flamand, Philippe and Emmanuelle Harros, Quidam de Revel, Frieder Roth, Eva Samama (Dressing d'Eva), Gilles Hamel and Carmen Lucini; along with Mylène Demongeot and Liliane Dreyfus for their kind welcome.

Jérôme Hanover would like to thank Farid Chenoune, Barbara Jeauffroy-Mairet, Florence Müller, Sarah Pialeprat, Jéromine Savignon, and Sinan Sigic for their assistance, their confidence, and their support of this project.

Photograph credits